Star

2

D1328455

SPORTS HEROES AND LEGENDS™

Cal Ripken Jr.

Read all of the books in this exciting,
action-packed biography series!

SPORTS HEROES AND LEGENDS™

Cal Ripken Jr.

by Matt Doeden

Twenty-First Century Books/Minneapolis

For Julia, Mitch, and Ayla

Twenty-First Century Books
A division of Lerner Publishing Group, Inc.
241 First Avenue North
Minneapolis, MN 55401 U.S.A.

Website address: www.lernerbooks.com

Cover photograph:
© Ronald C. Modra/Sports Imagery/Getty Images

Library of Congress Cataloging-in-Publication Data

Doeden, Matt.
    Cal Ripken, Jr. / by Matt Doeden.
        p.   cm. — (Sports heroes and legends)
    Includes bibliographical references and index.
    ISBN 978–0–8225–9040–8 (lib. bdg. : alk. paper)
    1. Ripken, Cal, 1960—Juvenile literature. 2. Baseball players—United States—Biography—Juvenile literature. 3. Baltimore Orioles (Baseball team)—Juvenile literature. I. Title.
GV865.R47D64 2009
796.357092—dc22 [B]   2007039338

Manufactured in the United States of America
1 2 3 4 5 6 – BP – 14 13 12 11 10 09

Contents

Prologue

Two Days in the Sun

At the beginning of the 1991 Major League Baseball season, many experts believed that Cal Ripken Jr.'s days as a star player were over. The former American League Most Valuable Player (MVP) and World Series champion had struggled badly over the past couple of seasons. The thirty-year-old shortstop was chasing down one of baseball's most celebrated records—Lou Gehrig's streak of 2,130 consecutive games played. Cal had played in more than 1,400 consecutive games and still looked strong and healthy. Yet his batting average in 1990 had been a career-low .250, and his power numbers—home runs and runs batted in—had dipped as well.

But in the first half of the season, Cal had proved his critics wrong. He led the league with a batting average of .348. Fans had voted him to start at shortstop for the American League in the All-Star Game at the SkyDome in Toronto, Ontario, Canada.

1

Cal traveled to Toronto for the two-day All-Star festivities. He was invited to take part in the annual home-run-hitting contest, which takes place the night before the actual game. Cal was almost embarrassed to be in the event—he wasn't known as a slugger and didn't think he could keep up with powerful swingers such as Cecil Fielder of the Detroit Tigers and Joe Carter of the Toronto Blue Jays. Nobody really thought he'd be much of a factor.

The eight-player contest featured four hitters from each league. Each player had a chance to hit as many home runs as he could before reaching ten "outs." (In a home run derby, any swing that does not result in a home run counts as an out.) The hitters were taking part in both a team and an individual competition. The four hitters on each team added their totals together to get a team total. The league with more homers was the contest winner. On top of that, the individual with the most home runs would be the derby champion.

Cal had to go first. He was the player with the lowest total of regular-season home runs coming into the contest. Observers expected that his turn at the plate wouldn't amount to anything more than a warm-up for the real power hitters. Even Cal wasn't looking to do much. He didn't want to alter his usual swing for fear that he would develop bad habits that would carry over when the regular-season resumed. Instead of swinging his hardest, he just tried to make solid contact and hoped to hit a few over the fence so that he didn't embarrass himself.

On his first swing, Cal hit a towering shot into the Skydome's deep center field. The ball sailed over the fence and into the area where the television cameras had been set up. *BOOM!* His next swing was another homer. *CRACK!* Another. The ball was flying off Cal's bat. The crowd roared as he kept launching line drives over the fence—at one point hitting seven home runs in a row! The highlight of the contest came when he blasted one of his homers so high it hit a skybox window on the fourth deck. By the end of the contest, Cal had hit 12 home runs on 22 swings. Nobody could come close to matching his impressive showing, and he became the first shortstop ever to win the contest. By comparison, the other seven hitters in the contest had combined for just 15 homers.

Everything was going Cal's way as the National League and American League teams hit the field the next night for the All-Star Game. "My confidence was so high, I had so much momentum, I honestly felt I was going to do something big in that game," Cal later wrote.

He was right. Cal stepped to the plate in the third inning against Dennis Martinez of the Montreal Expos. The National League held a 1–0 lead, but the American League had two runners on base. Cal picked up where he'd left off the day before by smashing one more long home run over the center-field fence. His blast gave the American League a 3–1 lead.

"I threw a slider that stayed up [in the strike zone]," Martinez later said. "You don't make mistakes like that, especially to Cal now. He's in some kind of groove."

The American League held on for a 4–2 win, and Cal earned Most Valuable Player honors for the game. His hot hitting continued into the second half of the season, and he was named the league's MVP for the second time in his career—eight years after he'd first earned the honor. Nobody was saying Cal's career was nearing its end anymore. He was the best shortstop in baseball, and he wasn't about to let anyone forget it.

Chapter One

Born into Baseball

From the time he was a child, Calvin Edward Ripken Jr. did everything he could to live up to his father's name. Born August 24, 1960, in Havre de Grace, Maryland, to Violet (Vi) and Cal Sr. (called Rip), Cal inherited more than just his father's name. He also got his dad's love of baseball and his dedicated work ethic.

The Ripken family loved baseball. Rip was a minor-league catcher in the Baltimore Orioles organization. Cal's uncle Bill was also a minor leaguer. Even Vi had been a star softball player in her younger days. Growing up surrounded by baseball, Cal, his sister, Ellen, and his two brothers (Fred and Bill) all loved the game.

Rip's professional baseball career began in 1957. He was slowly advancing through the Orioles' minor-league system at the time Cal Jr. was born. (Nearly all professional baseball players begin their careers in the minor leagues. As they develop their skills, they work their way up from league to league, facing better competition each time. The best players eventually get a chance to play in the major leagues.)

In 1960 Rip hit a career-best .281 with 74 runs batted in (RBI)—respectable offensive numbers for a catcher. But just as Rip seemed on his way to the big leagues, everything changed. In the spring of 1961, a foul tip hit him on his right shoulder. Rip tried to play through the pain, but it kept getting worse. He lost much of the strength in his right arm, which meant he could no longer throw out base runners. Although he tried to continue playing, his arm was never the same. Rip's big-league dreams had been dashed.

Cal's first experience playing organized baseball came at age eight. His team went 8–0 (eight wins, zero losses) for the season, and Cal made only one out in those eight games.

The young father had to decide how to spend the rest of his life. Unwilling to leave baseball behind, Rip chose to pursue a career in coaching. Minor-league coaches and their families have tough lives. The hours are long, the pay is modest, and the moves are almost constant. But Rip didn't want to leave the sport he loved.

The family tried to establish a home base in Aberdeen, Maryland, but life on the road dominated Cal's childhood. During the next eighteen years, the Ripkens lived in fourteen towns spread across ten different states. From South Dakota to Texas to Wisconsin, they were always on the move. North Carolina, New York, Virginia, Arkansas, Florida, Washington, and back home to Maryland—sometimes Cal's life felt like one long, continuous move. The only constant was baseball.

"When the children were not of school age, we would travel with Rip," recalled Vi. "I used to carry Cal in my arms to the ballpark."

With such nonstop change in his young life, it's little wonder why Cal felt most at home on a baseball diamond. Rip worked long hours, and if Cal wanted to spend time with his dad, his best bet was at the ballpark. The little boy loved the game and idolized the players his father coached. Future Oriole stars such as Jim Palmer played with the strong, energetic Cal and answered his constant stream of questions.

"[Cal] was always around the ballpark," recalled Brooks Robinson, a future Hall of Fame third baseman. "He lived and died baseball. I know guys are supposed to like baseball, but some are special."

BROOKS ROBINSON

One of Cal's childhood idols was Brooks Robinson, a standout third baseman for the Baltimore Orioles. Robinson, born in 1937 in Little Rock, Arkansas, debuted for the Orioles in 1955. He went on to play twenty-three seasons for the team. He was best known for his fielding and won sixteen straight Gold Glove awards from 1960 to 1975. His finest season was 1964, when his .317 batting average and 28 home runs earned him American League (AL) MVP honors. Robinson was elected to the Hall of Fame in 1983.

Little Cal showed his fierce competitive spirit at an early age. No matter the game, he didn't like to lose. For his family, his temper tantrums following a loss—at anything, from sports to card games—were almost legendary. He hated losing so much that he wasn't above cheating to win, according to his mother.

"I was always better than anyone else in my family when it came to sports," Cal remembered. "My two brothers and my sister liked to team up on me. If they ever beat me at anything, the whole house would have to hear about it. I didn't like that."

All of the moving made it hard for Cal Jr. to make friends. He often felt alone, with only his sister and brothers as friends. Sometimes he was so miserable that he would even try to sneak out of class to go home.

"Life on the road was tough on me and my brothers and sister," Cal wrote in his autobiography, *The Only Way I Know*. "By choice, maybe, but by necessity too, the Ripkens have always been pretty self-sufficient. We relied mainly on each other for friendship and activities."

Cal and his siblings broke so many windows in the Ripken home playing sports that their father made them learn how to cut and replace windows themselves.

By the time he was twelve, Cal was helping his dad's teams in any way he could. He served as the team's batboy and would "shag," or catch, fly balls during batting practice. He also joined a Little League team in Asheville, North Carolina. He started out following in his dad's footsteps as a catcher but soon switched to playing outfield and pitching. His talent was evident early on. At age thirteen, he led his Little League team to the state championship.

Cal was a talented pitcher, but he was wild. In one game, his pitches hit four batters in a row. His coach came to the mound to talk to his young star about the erratic throws. "They don't get out of the way very fast, do they?" the young pitcher told his coach.

Cal entered Aberdeen High School in 1974. While he was a good student, especially in math, baseball remained the center of his life. He tried out for—and made—the baseball team as a second baseman. Even though he struggled in his first year with the team, Cal was determined to achieve the goal he had set for himself by this time—to become a professional baseball player.

---

66 *Ever since Cal was old enough to talk, Cal always wanted to be a ballplayer. He always had a ball and glove in his hand.* 99

—Violet Ripken

In 1976, when Cal was in tenth grade, his father joined the Orioles' major-league coaching staff. It was a big career move for Rip, and it had serious benefits for Cal and his brothers. They got to hang out at Memorial Stadium, the home of the Orioles. Rip introduced Cal to shortstop Mark Belanger, who was happy to teach the talented youngster the ins and outs of the position.

Cal's blossoming talent didn't go unnoticed by those around him. Oriole manager Earl Weaver watched fifteen-year-old Cal taking batting practice. The next year, the Orioles invited Cal to a formal tryout, where he had a chance to show his skills to the Orioles coaches. All the exposure helped him make a big impression on his dad's bosses.

In 1977 Cal's high school coach asked him to pitch. Cal was up to the challenge. His performance on the mound and at the plate earned him the title of county MVP. Scouts from major-league teams were showing up at Aberdeen's games. Cal's future as a professional ballplayer was looking more and more realistic.

Chapter | Two

The Prospect

By Cal's senior year in high school, he had grown to a strong 6-foot-2, 185 pounds. His size and talent were getting him plenty of attention from major-league scouts. Most scouts who watched him play saw his future as a pitcher. After all, in his final season at Aberdeen High School, he went 7–2 (seven wins, two losses) with 100 strikeouts in just 60 innings. He dominated his competition in leading his team to the Class A state championship. In the title game, he'd thrown a two-hitter and struck out 17.

But one scout, Baltimore's Dick Bowie, thought Cal's future might be in the infield. His strong arm would be a defensive asset at shortstop or third base, and Cal was also an accomplished hitter, having batted .492 in his senior year.

Cal was also a clever player. He had used some creative tactics to lead his high school team to the state championship in

1978. For example, in the third inning of the championship game, Aberdeen trailed Thomas Stone High School 3–1. But a storm was coming. At the time, the rules stated that if the trailing team had finished fewer than three innings at bat, the game would be canceled and would start over at a later date. As the pitcher, Cal had some control over finishing that inning. Instead of moving the game forward, he stalled. Cal kept throwing to first base (to keep the runner from getting a big lead), knowing that if the rain came soon enough, the game wouldn't count. At one point, he threw to first base nine straight times. Sure enough, the rain started, and the game was canceled. A week later, Cal was back on the mound starting fresh with a score of 0–0. This time, there was no rain, and Aberdeen took the championship.

The spring of 1978 was a nervous, busy time for Cal. He'd always been a good student and was getting ready to graduate from high school with his classmates. Unlike many of his friends, however, Cal wasn't thinking about heading to college the following fall. Instead he was wondering in what round—and by whom—he would be selected in the 1978 amateur draft. Cal had no doubt he'd be drafted—plenty of scouts raved about his potential. But Cal had no control over where he'd end up playing. His preference, of course, was to join the Orioles' system. He'd grown up as an Oriole, after all, and the idea of one day sharing a dugout with his father was exciting. But part of Cal also wondered if it wouldn't be better if another team drafted him. Would people think the Orioles had drafted him just because of his father?

The question of how high he'd be drafted was also on his mind. While plenty of scouts liked him, a few had their doubts. One scout said he had a "lack of fluid mobility that will limit [his future]." Another pointed out that Cal "got high school hitters out with curveballs and didn't hit or run [well]."

Finally on June 6, 1978, draft day arrived. School wasn't even out yet. So when he got the news that the Orioles had selected him in the second round, with the 48th overall pick, it came from one of the school's office workers. Cal was an Oriole! He quickly signed a minor-league contract that called for a $20,000 bonus.

A week later, seventeen-year-old Cal joined his new team in Bluefield, West Virginia. The Bluefield Orioles (called the Baby Birds by fans) played in the Appalachian League—a league set up just for players in their first season of professional ball.

Cal's first game as a pro was forgettable. Playing before a mostly empty stadium, he looked overmatched at the plate and made three errors at shortstop. And this wasn't Cal's only tough night of that 1978 season. He soon learned that pro ball was a lot tougher than high school. But despite this, his team-mates marveled at his composure and his baseball knowledge.

"Cal stood out from the rest of the rookies," said teammate and future major leaguer Larry Sheets. "Because he had been around baseball all his life, he possessed a maturity we didn't have. He knew the lingo. He also knew how to separate the fun side of baseball from the business aspect of the game."

CAL AND LOU

The careers of Cal Ripken Jr. and Lou Gehrig will forever be linked. Like Ripken, the New York–born Gehrig was a man who showed up every day to play baseball. The Yankee, nicknamed the Iron Horse, played in 2,130 straight games from 1925 to 1939. The two-time MVP was finally sidelined by a disease called amyotrophic lateral sclerosis (ALS). Gehrig died in 1941, two years after his final game. Not long after, ALS became known as Lou Gehrig's disease.

Cal embraced the minor-league lifestyle—living on little money, traveling from small town to small town, and playing in front of sparse (and often rowdy) crowds. He and three teammates shared some rented rooms in Bluefield. The young players—Cal, Sheets, Tim Norris, and Mike Boddicker—were always together, playing cards or pool or just hanging out. But most of all, they lived for baseball. For Cal, it seemed, little had changed. In a way, he'd been living the minor-league life for most of his seventeen years.

❝Cal is a good student, a dedicated kid. He's dedicated to professional baseball. He's a workhorse and a hustler.❞

—BLUEFIELD MANAGER JUNIOR MINOR

As the season dragged on, Cal continued to struggle, especially in the field. For the season, he had 32 errors in just 63 games. People began questioning whether shortstop was the best position for him. With his tall, lean frame, he didn't fit the typical mold for a shortstop. At that time, smaller athletes with greater speed and agility dominated the majors. Cal continued to work hard on his defense, even though he knew that his future could be at third base—a less demanding defensive position.

Cal's struggles at the plate may have been even worse than his fielding woes. He batted just .264. That average would have been okay for a power hitter, but Cal didn't hit a single home run that season. Nothing was going right, and Cal's future in baseball was very much in doubt.

Cal entered the 1979 season knowing that he had to improve. If he didn't, his career could be over quickly. The eighteen-year-old reported to his new team in the Class A Florida State League. Cal was still growing, and he had added quite a bit of muscle to his frame during the off-season. The added strength paid off. Cal hit .303 with 5 home runs. He was even named to the league's all-star team. But questions about his position continued to follow him. Many in the Oriole organization were convinced he should switch to third base. In fact, in 1979, he played about half his games at shortstop and the other half at third base.

In August, Cal was called up (promoted) to Baltimore's Class AA team in Charlotte, North Carolina. He played only 17 games there before the season ended. He didn't hit for a good average but showed some power with 3 home runs.

Nineteen-year-old Cal, now 6-foot-4, 205 pounds, returned to Charlotte in the spring of 1980. His coaches there promptly made a decision—he was going to be the team's third baseman, not the shortstop. The switch allowed Cal to really focus on his hitting. That, combined with his larger, stronger frame, led to a power surge for the young infielder. After having hit just 8 home runs in his first two minor-league seasons, Cal exploded for 28 homers in 1980. That output, paired with a respectable .279 batting average, erased all suspicions that Cal was in the Oriole organization just because of his father. Far from it—Cal had become one of the hottest prospects in baseball.

By 1981 the Orioles were paying serious attention to the young infielder. Cal earned an invitation to spring training with the big-league team. But with Doug DeCinces playing third base almost every day, the Orioles had no real place for Cal. So the team sent him back to the minors—this time to their Class AAA (the highest level of the minor leagues) team in Rochester, New York.

THE GAME THAT WOULDN'T END

In 1981 Cal's AAA Rochester team played in one of the most unusual games in baseball history. Rochester took a lead in the ninth inning, but Pawtucket tied it to send the game into extra innings. The marathon was on. Nobody could score. Finally, in the top (first half) of the 21st inning, Rochester scored the go-ahead run. But Pawtucket tied it again in the bottom half of the inning.

The game just kept going. In inning number 32, Rochester had another potential run thrown out at home plate. The teams played on. Finally, after eight hours of play, the game was postponed. The teams resumed the game two months later. Pawtucket finally scored the winning run in the bottom of the 33rd inning. Cal went 2 for 13 (2 hits in 13 at bats) in the longest game in baseball history.

Cal didn't slow down a bit. On April 27, he blasted 3 home runs in a single game. In just 85 games (a few of which he started at shortstop), he hit 23 home runs and batted .288. Cal's future was looking brighter and brighter. Even the Orioles, who liked to bring young players slowly through the minor-league system, couldn't wait much longer. It was time for Cal to make his big-league dreams come true.

Chapter Three

The Big Show

On August 8, 1981, Cal got the news he'd waited for his whole life. The Orioles had called him up to Baltimore. The major-league players and owners had just gotten through a bitter labor dispute—including a players' strike that wiped out part of the season. But the strike was over and the games were back on. The Orioles were battling for a playoff spot, and they wanted Cal on the bench.

The news was both good and bad for Cal. He was thrilled to be joining the big-league team. But he knew that manager Earl Weaver wouldn't be using such a young, untested player very often with his team in the thick of a playoff race. For this reason, Cal's major-league debut wasn't quite what he'd imagined it would be. He didn't take the field at third base or shortstop. He didn't step to the plate for his first taste of big-league pitching. Instead, he entered his first game as a pinch runner.

The Orioles and the Kansas City Royals were tied in the twelfth inning. The slow-footed Ken Singleton doubled, and Weaver sent the speedier Cal to second base to pinch-run. The move paid off. John Lowenstein hit a solid single. Cal raced around third base (speeding past his father, who was the team's third-base coach) to score the winning run. The debut may not have been what Cal had envisioned, but he'd helped his team win an important game.

"When I was announced and went in as a pinch runner, it wasn't as big a thrill as I thought it would be," Cal said after the game. "I thought it would be at bat or in the field. Anyway, it happened so fast. . . . Once I went in, I was just trying to concentrate on the situation rather than be awed by it."

As expected, Cal played sparingly at the end of the 1981 season. He sat on the bench for days at a time, making it tough to find his rhythm at the plate when he did get in. By mid-September, he was hitting a miserable .128, and Weaver decided not to use him anymore. For the final three weeks, Cal was a spectator from the bench—his only action came as a pinch runner.

"[Sitting on the bench] was eating my insides out," Cal later said. "I told myself, 'If you get a shot to play, don't come out.'"

Because Cal had played so little in 1981, he was still considered a rookie (first-year player) in 1982. Weaver and the Orioles believed in the young infielder, and they showed their confidence by trading DeCinces to make room for Cal at third base.

A Ripken in the Wings

By 1981 Cal's younger brother Billy was attracting attention from major-league scouts. Billy excelled as a pitcher at Aberdeen, going two straight seasons without a loss. But like Cal, scouts saw Billy as a future infielder. The Orioles drafted him in the eleventh round of the 1982 amateur draft.

Despite his struggles and limited action in 1981, the expectations for twenty-one-year-old Cal were high in 1982. On opening day—April 6—against the Royals, he seemed ready to fulfill them all. Cal stepped to the plate with Singleton on base. Right-hander Dennis Leonard delivered a pitch that Cal liked, and he cracked the ball high and far. It sailed over the fence, giving Baltimore an early lead and sending the 52,000 Oriole fans in attendance into a frenzy. Cal ended the game 3 for 5 and played a big role in the Orioles' 13–5 victory.

The memory of Cal's impressive opening day quickly faded, however. The rookie suddenly dropped into a terrible slump. By the beginning of May, he was just 7 for 60 for a terrible average of .118. He was miserable. "I just couldn't hit the ball, and I didn't know why," Cal later wrote.

Cal's dad watched his son struggle. "Almost all young hitters go through this same thing," he said. "They go into a little slump and they go to the plate trying to get a hit instead of trying to hit the ball. . . . Ninety percent of batting slumps are caused by your mental approach, and that's what Cal is fighting now."

The fans and the media were losing patience with Cal. Rumors swirled that Weaver would soon bench him or even send him back to the minors. Cal's coaches and teammates all did their best to help the struggling youngster. Everyone had advice on how to change his stance or his swing or the strategy he used against opposing pitchers. But none of it helped. Cal, more confused than ever because of all the advice, just struggled more and more.

Help ended up coming from an unexpected source—an opposing player. The Orioles were playing the California Angels. Future Hall of Famer Reggie Jackson got a chance to talk to Cal while standing on third base. The friendly Jackson—a former Oriole—had heard all about Cal's struggles. He told the young third baseman, "Don't let everyone else tell you how to hit. You could hit before you got [to the big leagues]. Just be yourself and hit the way you want to hit."

Something clicked with Cal, and he took Jackson's advice to heart. The next day, Cal got two hits. After the second hit, he looked into the Angels' dugout to see Jackson laughing and nodding to him. The slump was over. Talk of Weaver benching his young infielder quickly disappeared.

Cal bought his first house in Cockeysville, Maryland, which is about thirty minutes from the Orioles' Memorial Stadium.

At the time, the doubleheader Cal and the Orioles played against the Toronto Blue Jays on May 29 didn't seem like anything special. Cal played the first game, then rested on the bench for the second—a common occurrence in baseball. But it was the last game of the 1982 season that Cal would watch from the dugout. Nobody knew it at the time, but Cal's legendary streak was about to begin.

Few people remember that Cal started his streak as a third baseman. That's because on July 1, 1982, Weaver decided that Cal could help the team more as a shortstop. Unlike most people with the Orioles, Weaver had always envisioned Cal as a shortstop, even if he didn't have the typical build for the position.

Nobody of Cal's size had ever excelled as a shortstop. Even Cal himself wondered if Weaver might be making a mistake. But Cal wasn't one to complain. As long as his name was on the lineup card, he was happy to take the field.

Baltimore's season as a team was a lot like Cal's individual year—early struggles followed by a late-season surge. Cal and Eddie Murray—the team's brightest young stars—led the charge, which included a stretch that saw the team go 33–10 and climb into the thick of the AL East divisional race. Cal was playing great in the field and at the plate. In late August, he earned AL Player of the Week honors. On September 14, he hit his first career grand slam (off of Yankee pitcher Mike Morgan).

EDDIE MURRAY

Murray, nicknamed "Steady Eddie," was one of the best players and friends that Cal ever played with. Murray, born in Los Angeles in 1956, came up with the Orioles in 1977 and earned AL Rookie of the Year honors. Murray spent time with the Dodgers, Mets, Indians, and Angels before he retired in 1997. When he retired, he was one of only four players in baseball history to collect 3,000 or more career hits and 500 or more home runs. He was elected to the Hall of Fame in 2003.

Entering the final weekend of the season, the Orioles trailed the Milwaukee Brewers by three games. The two teams were set to play a season-ending four-game series at Memorial Stadium. The Orioles had to win all four games to claim the division title. It was a long shot—beating a good Brewer team four straight times seemed close to impossible. But a long shot was better than no shot at all. The Orioles fans were excited, and the team had some extra incentive to win—Weaver had announced his retirement at the end of the season. The players badly wanted to make the playoffs for their legendary manager.

Cal and the Orioles only increased the level of excitement, winning the first two games. Then in the third game, they crushed the Brewers 11–3. The teams were tied for first place with one game to play! The Oriole fans packed the stadium for the deciding game, eager for a celebration. But Baltimore couldn't manage the unlikely sweep. Milwaukee won the final game 10–2 and advanced to the playoffs. Baltimore's season was over.

Cal's impressive first full season earned him plenty of attention. His .264 batting average, 28 home runs, and 93 RBIs were tremendous numbers for a rookie infielder. Baseball fans argued over whether he or Minnesota's Kent Hrbek should win Rookie of the Year honors. Hrbek, a first baseman, had batted .301 with 23 home runs and was one of the finest fielding first basemen in the league. Cal was hopeful, but he certainly wasn't expecting the honor. Still, the baseball writers who voted for the award saw something special in Cal. Because he played short-stop, a more-demanding defensive position and one from which such power numbers are rare, they overwhelmingly voted him the American League's rookie of the year.

"I was surprised by the margin [of votes]," Cal said. "Hrbek had a fabulous year and I got off to a poor start. I figured that I had a legitimate chance, but I thought it would be close. . . . [Winning] was a relief to me more than anything. . . . I felt like I was setting myself up for a big letdown."

Individual honors were great, but what Cal really craved was team success. In 1983 he and his teammates had their sights set on a goal they'd almost achieved in 1982—an AL East title and a playoff berth.

In 1983 Cal and Eddie Murray made a bet on who would have more strikeouts. Cal lost, striking out 97 times to Murray's 90, and had to buy his friend a nice dinner.

Joe Altobelli took over as the Orioles' manager in 1983. Just as Weaver had done, Altobelli wrote Cal's name on the lineup card every day. It wasn't a hard decision. Cal never wanted a day off, and he played so well that his team needed him every game. In fact, Cal didn't just play every game of the 1983 season; he played every *inning*!

The 1983 Orioles were an interesting team. Old was meeting new. A generation of Oriole greats—Jim Palmer, Singleton, Rich Dauer, and others—were on the tail ends of their careers. Meanwhile, a group of young players, including Cal and Eddie Murray, were beginning a youth movement in Baltimore. Usually veterans carry a team. But for the 1983 season, Baltimore's youngsters didn't need any carrying. Ripken and Murray were the featured attractions.

Cal's great play earned him a trip to his first All-Star Game. "I felt I was good enough to be there," he said of the honor. "But I was looking around the locker room at the guys I used to root for. You sit there and talk to yourself and say, 'Oh God, how do I belong in this group?' and you say, 'I'm here, aren't I? I must belong.'"

The hits kept coming in the second half of the season. Cal drilled a grand slam against the Oakland A's on July 13. A week later, his four-hit performance against the Seattle Mariners helped propel the Orioles into first place. "Cal took the American League by storm in 1983," said teammate Rich Dempsey.

Cal wasn't the only one either—Murray was also enjoying a good season. As fall approached, the teammates had emerged as the leading candidates for the AL MVP award. Behind their great play, the Orioles kept winning. By season's end, they had clinched the AL East. They were headed to the playoffs!

Baltimore faced the Chicago White Sox in the American League Championship Series (ALCS). The teams would play a best-of-five series, meaning the first to win three games would advance to the World Series. Chicago won the first game 2–1, with Cal's ninth-inning single driving in Baltimore's only run. But the Orioles came back to win the next three, led by Cal's stellar .400 batting average in the four games. Cal and his teammates celebrated. They were going to face the Philadelphia Phillies in the World Series!

The pressure kept building. Cal was especially excited to play in front of President Ronald Reagan, who was in attendance for game one in Baltimore. "It's the same game it always is," Cal said of the pressure. "But I looked up [in the stands] and I wanted to see the president."

Game one didn't go as planned for the home team. The Phillies won 2–1 to take the lead in the best-of-seven series. But the Orioles weren't discouraged—they'd come back strong after losing the first game to Chicago in the ALCS. And just as they had against the White Sox, the Orioles steamrolled the Phillies in the next four games, winning game two in Baltimore (Cal contributed an RBI single to the win), then sweeping the

Phillies in Philadelphia to win the series 4–1. The Orioles were world champions!

The series highlight for Cal came in game 5. With two outs in the bottom of the ninth inning, he caught a line drive off the bat of Garry Maddox to record the final out. Cal squeezed the ball tightly as his teammates stormed onto the field. In just his second full season in the majors, Cal was a World Series champion! He hadn't had a great series at the plate, managing just 3 singles in 18 at bats for a .167 average, but his defense was solid.

"By far, the best moment of my big league career was when I caught the last out at the World Series," Cal later said. "Of all the great things that had happened, catching the last out at the World Series and having that feeling of satisfaction and fulfillment that comes over you at that moment, none of those other individual moments come close to [that]."

A crowd of 250,000 people lined the streets of Baltimore when the Orioles returned for a victory parade. The biggest cheers were reserved for Cal and Eddie Murray. In the final months of the season, the debate over who should be the AL MVP had intensified. Cal had finished the regular season with a .318 batting average, 27 home runs, and 102 RBIs. Murray's numbers were very similar—an average of .306, 33 home runs, and 111 RBIs. On the surface, the numbers seemed to favor

Murray. But once again, it wasn't as simple as that. Murray was a first baseman, while Cal was a shortstop. Just as voters had taken position into account in the voting for the 1982 Rookie of the Year award, they did so for the 1983 AL MVP award. Cal was thrilled to learn that he'd beaten out his teammate and friend in a very close vote.

In the voting for the 1983 AL MVP award, Cal received 322 points. Murray received 290 points. Carlton Fisk of the White Sox came in third place, with 209 points.

One year after winning Rookie of the Year, Cal was the league MVP! That had never happened in major league history (although in 1975, Fred Lynn of the Boston Red Sox won both awards in the same season). Once again, however, the award wasn't without controversy. Many fans believed that the baseball writers had unfairly penalized Murray because he didn't have a friendly relationship with the media. But plenty of fans and experts defended the selection. Cal had played every inning of every game, and at a very demanding position. The offensive numbers told only part of the story.

> ❝I did my share for the team. I pulled my load this year. But so did all the players. I could share the MVP with the whole team, and I will.❞
>
> —CAL RIPKEN JR.[22]

Murray didn't have any hard feelings. "I feel like [Cal] deserves it," he told reporters. "I hope he does it again and the Orioles win the world championship again. . . . I know of no better teammate and friend than Cal Ripken."

Chapter Four

In the Spotlight

By the beginning of the 1984 season, Cal's consecutive games streak was at 280. Even more impressive, he hadn't missed a single inning during the streak. Still, no one thought he would challenge Gehrig's famous record. Something as simple as an illness or a twisted ankle could end it.

Yet nothing stopped Cal from doing his job every day. The Orioles rewarded his dedication and brilliant play with a four-year, $4-million contract. Cal responded by giving back to the community, donating 2,000 Orioles tickets to children who would not otherwise get the chance to see the team in person. With a World Series ring and an MVP trophy, Cal understood that he had become a role model to thousands of kids. He was determined to be a good one.

"I recognize that as a baseball player, I am a public celebrity, and willingly or not, I am a role model for many, especially youth,"

Cal said. "I take this responsibility very seriously. . . . It may be a burden, but if people perceive me as a good role model and I feel I contribute to their lives, then I'm happy and gratified."

❝It was always a privilege to watch Cal play, especially with Eddie and Cal Jr. together. It didn't matter if you were playing beside them or watching them on the bench, it was a privilege to watch them play.**❞**

—ORIOLE OUTFIELDER JOHN LOWENSTEIN[28]

Cal enjoyed another great season individually in 1984. One of the highlights of his year came on May 6 against the Texas Rangers. Cal opened the game with three hits—a single, a double, and a triple. He was a home run away from completing "the cycle," one of the rarest achievements in baseball.

In the ninth inning, Cal stepped to the plate for what would almost certainly be his final at bat. He was aware that a homer would give him the cycle, but he would later insist that he wasn't trying to complete the feat. "Maybe in the on-deck circle [I thought] it'd be nice," he said. "But when you get to the plate, you just think of hitting the ball hard."

Cal did exactly that, driving a pitch over the fence. He'd done it! Cal had become only the second Oriole to hit for the cycle. (Brooks Robinson had done it in 1960—a month before Cal was born.)

From August 29 to September 1, 1984, Cal reached base safely eleven straight times. He got seven hits and drew four walks during the stretch.

Cal was playing great, but things weren't going so well for the Orioles. The team could only watch helplessly as the Detroit Tigers exploded to an amazing 35–5 start, all but burying Baltimore (and everyone else in the AL East) before June even rolled around. Cal made the All-Star team, batted .304, and belted 27 home runs. He also set an American League record with 583 defensive assists. (An infielder gets an assist for fielding a ball and throwing a runner out.) But all of his efforts weren't enough. Baltimore finished the season with an 85–77 record and in distant fifth place. For Cal, his teammates, and the Orioles' fans, fifth place was a huge disappointment for a team that had won the World Series the year before.

Things didn't improve in 1985. The Orioles stumbled out of the gate and could never get on a serious winning streak. By midseason, Altobelli had been fired, and Weaver came out of retirement to take over as manager.

Cal Sr. spent one game as the Orioles interim (temporary) manager after Altobelli was fired. The Orioles won the game, and Weaver took over the next day.

Cal's consecutive games streak was in serious danger early in the season. On April 10, Cal was in the field, holding a runner at second base (playing close to the bag to prevent the runner from taking a big lead). Pitcher Mike Boddicker spun and fired the ball to Cal in an attempt to pick off the runner. A spike on Cal's shoe caught the edge of the base. His ankle buckled and the twenty-four-year-old shortstop cried out in pain. But despite a noticeable limp, he finished the inning, got the ankle taped in the dugout, and returned to the field. Even though the ankle swelled badly, the injury didn't force him to miss a single inning.

"[For Cal,] it's a mental thing as well as physical," said teammate Fred Lynn of Cal's ability to play through pain. "No question, he is blessed physically, but he's got a high mental [toughness] as well."

By the end of 1985, the streak had grown to 603 games, and Cal still hadn't missed an inning. He batted .282 with 25 home runs. But the Orioles managed a record of just 83–79, fourth in the AL East.

Since the World Series title in 1983, the Orioles had gone through a steady decline. The team was still a winner—even if it was only a few games over .500. (A .500 team wins and loses the same amount of games.) That changed in 1986. Even the return of Earl Weaver wasn't enough to save the team from a bitterly disappointing finish. Cal was one of the few bright spots for Oriole fans. Murray was involved in a disagreement with ownership, lost time to an injury, and fell out of favor with the fans. Cal, meanwhile, was out on the field every day, giving his all. But the team around him struggled badly. A stream of injuries combined with a struggling pitching staff to make for a long, difficult summer.

❝ *Cal did not have the range that some other shortstops had, but he had a very strong arm, knew the hitters well, and knew how to position himself.* **❞**
—Former Oriole Bobby Grich on Cal's defense

A game on August 6 typified the season. The Orioles achieved an extremely rare feat by hitting two grand slams in the same inning. But still, somehow, the team managed to lose the game. For Baltimore fans, the game perfectly summed up a lost season. The Orioles wound up with a 73–89 record, putting them in last place in the division and giving the franchise its first losing record since 1967.

Fortunately for Cal, the on-field misery wasn't following him off the field. By 1986 he had a serious girlfriend—Kelly Geer. Cal and Kelly had met in a strange way. One night at a restaurant, a married couple—Joan and Robert Geer—had spotted Cal and walked over to meet the star shortstop. Cal had signed an autograph for their daughter Kelly, who was Cal's age. Cal scribbled his name on a napkin, with a short message. It read, "To Kelly, if you look anything like your mother, I'm sorry I missed you." Later, when her parents gave Kelly the autograph, she responded by saying, "That's great, Mom, but who is he?"

DRIBBLE AND SHOOT

Like Cal, Kelly was an athlete growing up. Years earlier, she had finished second in the state's "Dribble and Shoot" contest, which tests a player's basketball skills. Cal was impressed. He'd entered the same contest as a kid and had never gotten far. Kelly joked that her trophy and her height (she's almost six feet tall) were what attracted Cal to her, because he wanted sons who would be basketball players.

A few months later, Kelly saw Cal at a restaurant. She walked up to him and thanked him for the autograph. The two talked and quickly hit it off. Soon they were inseparable. On December 31, 1986, Cal asked Kelly to marry him. She accepted and the couple began planning a wedding for the following November.

Cal was thrilled. And it wasn't the only good news he got during that off-season. Weaver had returned to retirement, and the Orioles announced his replacement as manager—Cal Sr.! Cal was going to be playing for his father!

Chapter Five

Team Ripken

Father and son proudly took the field to open the 1987 season. But despite the excitement, they also were realistic. The Orioles hadn't been a good team in 1986, and they had little reason to believe they'd be much better in 1987.

"Rip was fully aware of the shortcomings of the Orioles team he was invited to manage," Vi said. "But he never hesitated. In life, when you get the opportunity, you have to take it."

The season began with a familiar pattern. Cal excelled, but the team struggled. At one point, Cal was 14 for 27 when hitting with runners in scoring position (runners at second or third base). He was leading the league in most offensive categories, including his .341 batting average, and his defense was as solid as ever. Even so, the Orioles couldn't seem to compete in the tough AL East. By July 4, they were 31–49 and had lost 29 of their last 34 games.

While pitching was Baltimore's main problem, poor play at second base had also been a problem. The Orioles decided to try a new, younger player at the position. On July 11, the team called up that player—Billy Ripken. Cal was going to get a chance to play with his brother! It was the first time in baseball history that a father had managed two of his sons at the same time.

Billy was excited but realistic. "This is my dream," he said. "But I will not stay here just because I want to stay here or it looks good in the papers. I have gotten my shot, and I have to do something with it."

 Sports Illustrated featured the three Ripkens on its cover for one of its spring 1987 issues.

Oriole fans were excited to have yet another Ripken to cheer for, but they didn't fool themselves into believing they had a younger version of Cal. Billy was an excellent fielder with a sure glove and an accurate throwing arm, but he lacked his older brother's pop with the bat. In his first game, the Orioles lost 2–1 to the Minnesota Twins. Billy and Cal combined to go 0 for 7 in the loss.

Despite the poor debut, Billy was able to spark the struggling Orioles. He hit his first home run on July 19, and for a while, the team was red hot. On July 24, Cal's eighth-inning sacrifice fly drove in the winning run against the Kansas City Royals—the eleventh-straight win for the Orioles.

After years of struggling, excitement over the Orioles was high. But the hot streak didn't last. The team soon returned to its losing ways. Nobody was struggling more than Cal. He had fallen into a terrible slump. By August his consecutive games streak stood at 833, while his consecutive innings streak was an amazing 8,058. Fans were beginning to wonder if all of those innings were wearing down the twenty-six-year-old. Perhaps it was time for Cal to take a day off, critics said.

"I don't want to hear it," Cal replied. "When I'm not hitting, everybody says: 'He's tired; he needs a day off.' I wonder what excuse they would use if I took a day off and was still in a slump."

Finally, on September 14, the consecutive innings streak came to an end in Toronto. Cal was on base when the eighth inning ended. Normally someone would bring his glove onto the field for him for the next half inning. But when Billy grabbed his brother's glove, his dad told him to put it down. The Orioles were getting blown out 17–3. Cal was going to sit out the ninth inning. His consecutive innings streak ended at 8,243.

"I've been thinking about [resting Cal] for a long time," Rip said. "It was my decision, not his."

A little more than a week later, Cal got an even longer rest—although this time, it wasn't on purpose. In the first inning, Cal was called out on strikes by umpire Tim Welke. Cal disagreed with the strike call and said something to Welke. Whatever he said, Welke didn't appreciate it. The umpire ejected Cal from the game. But the consecutive games streak lived on. Cal had played in the game, even if it had been for only one inning.

For many reasons, 1987 was one of Cal's most disappointing seasons in baseball. The Orioles were terrible, finishing 67–95. Although he hit 27 home runs, Cal's .252 batting average was much lower than he expected of himself.

That off-season was filled with highs and lows for Cal and Kelly. They celebrated their November 13 wedding with friends and family. But they also had reason to worry. Kelly was diagnosed with a condition called Graves' disease. She had terrible headaches and fainting spells. She lost her appetite and dropped twenty-five pounds. The disease affected her immune system, but it was treatable. Doctors got her on the medications she needed, and her condition immediately improved. The couple had gone through a scare, but Kelly was going to be all right. Cal was free to focus his attention on the upcoming 1988 season.

After their wedding, Cal and Kelly moved into a fifteen-room mansion in a suburb of Baltimore.

Cal had plenty to look forward to in 1988. He, his dad, his brother, and the rest of the team were eager to improve on their dismal 1987. The local and national media reported rumors of moving the twenty-seven-year-old Cal to third base. But he ultimately remained at shortstop.

The season started disastrously with a 12–0 loss to the Brewers. By April 12—six games into the young season—the Orioles were 0–6. That day Cal was driving to Memorial Stadium for a game. He had the radio on and heard some shocking news—his father had been fired! He could barely believe what he was hearing. No manager in baseball history had been fired so early in the year. Frank Robinson was taking over as the team's manager.

"I felt deeply for my father," Cal later wrote. "He had been a loyal Oriole man for more than three decades. I couldn't imagine how painful being fired must have been for him."

For Cal and Billy, the situation was awkward. Their loyalty was split between their father and their team. Neither player agreed with what the organization had done, but they also wanted to remain loyal to their teammates and their new manager. So they kept quiet and just went about their jobs.

Billy batted an impressive .308 in 58 big-league games in 1987. But in 1988, he struggled badly, batting a dismal .207.

Anyone who thought that changing managers would be the solution to Baltimore's woes was in for a cold dose of reality. The team lost its first game under Robinson—6-1 to the Royals. It only got worse from there. Soon the team was a laughable 0-10.

Cal wasn't laughing. Twelve games into the season, he was 2 for 43 for an embarrassing .047 batting average. At one point, he went hitless in 19 straight at bats. And although Cal began to turn things around two weeks into the season, the team didn't follow his lead. The losing streak grew to an unbelievable 15 games—a major league record to start a season. It was officially the worst start any team in baseball history had suffered through.

"We were pathetic," said pitcher Scott McGregor. "We were the laughingstock of the town."

Setting a new record for futility wasn't enough, though. The losing streak just wouldn't seem to end. The Orioles couldn't do anything right. Their pitching was terrible. They couldn't get runners on base. And when they did, they never seemed to get a big hit to drive them in. Mistakes piled on top of mistakes as the streak grew to 18 games, then to 20. Entering the 22nd game of the season against the Chicago White Sox, Baltimore's record was 0–21. Finally, on April 29, Cal's four hits—including a home run—lifted the Orioles to a desperately needed 9–0 victory. The losing streak was finally over!

After the game, Cal wasn't looking for congratulations. "I'm not in a celebrating-type mood," he said. "One and twenty-one. That's not good. That's not a reason to be jumping around and celebrating."

 On July 27, 1988, Cal signed a three-year, $6-million contract extension with the Orioles.

Indeed, 1988 offered few chances for the Oriole players and fans to feel good. The team lost its final game in April to drop to 1–22—the worst single month any team had ever endured in Major League Baseball.

One of the few highlights for Cal in 1988 came on June 25, when his consecutive games streak grew to 1,000—almost halfway to Gehrig's famous mark. But as exciting as that may have been, the game was just another loss for the Orioles, this time 10–3. The team finished the year at 54–107, dead last in the division. Cal's numbers were fair—a .264 batting average with 23 home runs. But all told, it was a season he'd rather forget.

Chapter Six

Redemption

One of the great things about baseball—and all sports—is that there's always next year. For Cal, that was never more true than after the disaster of 1988. On opening day 1989, the Orioles were no longer the worst team in baseball. Like everyone else, they were 0–0. The slate was wiped clean.

The Orioles opened the season at home against the Boston Red Sox and the league's best pitcher—Roger Clemens (nicknamed the Rocket). Facing Clemens was a tall task for Cal and the Orioles, and by the sixth inning, they trailed 3–1. That inning, Cal stepped to the plate with two runners on base. He looked out to Clemens, wondering what the Rocket might throw. Clemens had struck out Cal on a 100-mile-per-hour fastball earlier in the game, so with a 2-2 count (two balls and two strikes), Cal was ready for Clemens's "heater." Cal lifted his front leg and took his best cut at the pitch. *CRACK!* Cal connected with the fastball. A packed Memorial Stadium erupted as the ball sailed over the fence for a home run. When Cal crossed home plate, the Orioles were ahead 4–3. They held on for a 5–4 victory. The year before, nearly a month had passed before the team had earned its first win. In 1989 the Orioles had beaten Roger Clemens on opening day!

"[Clemens] is one of the best pitchers in the game," Cal said. "The fans are going wild. You get that feeling. You could almost sense this season would be different."

CLUBHOUSE CHANGES

In 1989 Cal Sr. returned to the Baltimore coaching staff. Billy, Cal, and their dad were together once again. But Cal's friend and longtime teammate Eddie Murray was gone. The Orioles had traded him to the Los Angeles Dodgers.

Despite the dramatic win, virtually nobody predicted success for the young Orioles. After all, they'd been one of baseball's all-time worst teams in 1988, and Murray was gone. In addition, the team had a whopping thirteen rookies. All indications pointed to another season filled with struggles. But it didn't happen that way. Even though Cal didn't enjoy his best season statistically, the Orioles were somehow finding a way to win. By July they were in first place with a seven-game lead over the Toronto Blue Jays.

The team stumbled in the second half of the season, losing eight in a row at one point (one loss short of a record for a first-place team). Toronto soon passed Baltimore for first place.

Cal's consecutive games streak almost ended on August 7. After the first two Oriole hitters were called out on strikes by umpire Drew Coble, Cal came to the plate. After two called strikes (both of which Cal believed were balls), Cal turned to Coble to complain. The conversation between player and umpire quickly became heated. Cal was furious. Coble ejected the twenty-seven-year-old shortstop, but Cal kept going, inching closer and closer to the umpire. Robinson and Cal Sr. both rushed onto the field to grab their star, who was getting very close to bumping Coble—grounds for a suspension that would have ended Cal's consecutive games streak. Still angry, Cal tried to push past his dad to get at Coble again. But Robinson and the on-deck hitter, Keith Moreland, helped the elder Ripken restrain his son. Their efforts almost certainly saved Cal from a suspension. Coble later said that Cal had given him no choice but to toss him out of the game.

By August 31, Toronto and Baltimore were tied atop the AL East. But again, the Orioles stumbled, allowing the Blue Jays to regain the division lead. Cal did all he could to keep the Blue Jays within sight. On September 5, his 20th home run of the season gave the Orioles a 3–1 win over the Cleveland Indians. On September 11, he homered and drove in three runs to lead Baltimore to a 6–2 victory over the White Sox.

❝Not only is [Cal] an outstanding shortstop but he can hit the ball for power. I don't know how in the world he keeps going. He plays a tough position, a position where you can get hurt, and he just stays in there and does his job.❞

—Two-time AL Manager of the Year Lou Piniella

Entering the final weekend of the season, the Orioles trailed the Blue Jays by just a single game. And if that wasn't enough drama, the teams were scheduled to wind up the regular season with a three-game series against each other. That series would decide the division title. Baltimore needed to sweep Toronto to win the division outright or win two of the three games to tie the Blue Jays and force a one-game, winner-take-all playoff.

The first game was a tight pitchers' duel, but the Blue Jays held on for a 2–1 victory. Another one-run loss, this time 4–3, eliminated the Orioles the next day. Their playoff hopes were dead. But for a team that had lost 107 games the previous year, an 87–75 record and second place were amazing accomplishments. Even though it wasn't Cal's finest season statistically (he batted .257 and hit just 21 home runs), the team was better, and that's what really mattered. Cal could feel good going into the off-season.

Two months later, Kelly gave Cal an even better reason to feel good, giving birth to the couple's first child. When Rachel Marie Ripken was born November 22, 1989, Cal knew his life would never be the same.

"As you grow older, you find out that there's other things as important as baseball," he said. "The latest example is life. The whole secret of life is life itself. Life is totally different when you have a baby. You rearrange your priorities."

Cal and the Orioles took a big step backward in 1990. Early in the season, the team was losing, and Cal was mired in a deep slump. The Oriole fans were getting impatient. Despite the team's surprising performance in 1989, the fans were tired of watching their team lose. They expected more from the players they loved. Because Cal was the face of the team and its highest-paid player, he took a lot of the blame for the struggles. At one time, Cal could seem to do no wrong in the eyes of the fans. But his declining numbers had finally made him a target. Some fans suggested that Cal hadn't done enough in the final few weeks of 1989 and that his lack of production was the reason Baltimore had lost the division to Toronto. And the team was back to its losing ways. He was beginning to hear something he wasn't used to from his home fans—boos.

WORKING OUT

In 1990 Cal built a gym next to his house. It included a batting cage, a weight room, a basketball court, and more. Many of his teammates would come over to work out and play a game of hoops. Cal hoped that having a gym right there at home would keep him in top physical condition.

On June 11, Cal tied Everett Scott for second place on the all-time consecutive games list (with 1,307). The moment should have been a time for celebration. But after yet another strikeout in what had become an extended slump, the Oriole fans heartily booed him. The next day, when the team's public address announcer told the crowd that Cal was alone in second place on the list, trailing only Gehrig, they booed again.

"I was as frustrated as I've ever been," Cal later said. "I was at rock bottom, thinking I might be through [in the major leagues]."

Despite his struggles at the plate (his average was hovering just above .200), Cal's defense was getting noticed. For much of his career, critics had said that he wasn't suited for shortstop. But at one point in 1990, he went 95 straight games and 431 chances (defensive plays) without an error. Both were records for a shortstop.

"Mentally, you start to question yourself. Your confidence is such a roller coaster that whenever you go into a slump, psychologically, you start to think, 'Is this a trend that will continue for the rest of your career?'"

—CAL ON HIS STRUGGLES IN 1990

Still, Cal's hitting was all most people wanted to talk about. With his average at a terrible .209, he decided to change his batting stance, moving his feet farther apart and bending his knees more. The minor adjustment worked, and Cal started hitting again. By season's end, he had managed to lift his average to .250—still a career low, but a lot better than it had been at midseason. He added 21 home runs. His fielding percentage of .996, meanwhile, was another major league record. The most important statistic, however, was the team's 76–85 record, good for just fifth place in the division. After the hope that 1989 had brought, the season could only be described as a bitter failure.

Was Cal's career reaching its end? With each season, his numbers just kept dropping and dropping. He was almost 800 games away from Gehrig's record, but could he play well enough to stay in the lineup every day? Or would the former league MVP have to be benched? The 1991 season, Cal knew, would be pivotal. Even Cal wasn't sure anymore that he had what it took.

 Billy enjoyed his best season in 1990, batting .291 with 3 home runs and 48 runs scored.

Cal entered the 1991 season at thirty years of age. Most players reach their prime at around age twenty-seven. There didn't seem to be much reason to believe that Cal could improve significantly on his recent seasons.

The team struggled to an 11–19 start, and the organization responded by firing Robinson and replacing him with Johnny Oates. While Oates couldn't help the team turn things around, Cal caught fire under his leadership. Highlighted by a 6-for-10 day in a June 23 doubleheader against the Royals, Cal surged to a league-leading batting average of .348 at the All-Star break. The Orioles weren't doing well as a team, but Cal had answered the questions about his future. He was still one of the game's best, and he drove that point home with his amazing performance at the All-Star Game and the home-run contest.

The second half of the 1991 season went much as the first half did. Cal was on fire, but the Orioles struggled. On July 19, Cal cracked his 20th home run of the season, becoming just the eighth player in history to hit 20 home runs or more in each of his first 10 seasons. That same game, his famous streak grew to 1,500 games.

 From 1986 to 1991, the Orioles lost more games than any other team in baseball.

Two months later, Cal hit home run number 30 for the season. At the time, only three shortstops—Ernie Banks, Rico Petrocelli, and Vern Stephens—had managed that feat. By season's end, Cal had socked 34 dingers and batted a then-career-best .323. The postseason awards rained down on the thirty-one-year-old. He won his first Gold Glove as the league's best fielding shortstop. And even better, he earned his second

MVP trophy, becoming the first AL player ever to win the award while playing for a losing team. (The Orioles finished the season 67–95 and in sixth place.) That fact made Cal's selection controversial. Once again, people questioned whether he deserved the award. Critics pointed out that with or without Cal, the Orioles were a sixth-place team. But the voters disagreed. His numbers were almost unheard of for a shortstop, and he had done all he could to help his team.

"It was a storybook season," Cal said of 1991. "It seemed like whenever I was out there on the field, I could do no wrong. Very rarely do you get that feeling as an athlete. . . . I don't know if I'll ever be able to duplicate what I did this year. I never had a slump. Everything I hit seemed to fall in." The talk of Cal's career nearing its end was officially over.

Chapter Seven

Iron Man

Opening day of 1992 opened a new chapter in Oriole history. Gone were the familiar confines of Memorial Stadium, Cal's baseball home for more than ten years. The team moved to a new ballpark called Oriole Park at Camden Yards. The new ballpark, praised nationwide for its beauty and fan-friendly nature, would go on to inspire a new generation of ballparks.

The Orioles broke in their new stadium in style, with a 2–0 opening-day victory. But despite the win and the new stadium, many of the headlines were focused on something that was happening off the field: Cal's contract negotiations. He was scheduled to become a free agent after the 1992 season, meaning he would have the option of signing with any team that wanted him.

Oriole fans couldn't imagine their star in any other uniform. But talks between Cal and the organization dragged on and on.

Cal Ripken Jr. *(right)* and his father, Cal Ripken Sr., share a few moments together before an Orioles game at Yankee Stadium in 1982.

The Baltimore Orioles celebrate their World Series win in 1983.

Cal watches Orioles training camp in Miami, Florida, with his dad, Cal Sr. *(center),* and his brother Billy *(left)* in 1987.

Cal follows through on a home run during the home run contest on All-Star Weekend in 1991. He went on to win the contest with a total of twelve homers.

AP Photo/James Finley

Cal holds the Most Valuable Player trophy that was awarded to him at the All-Star Game in 1991.

Cal poses with his wife, Kelly *(right)*, and children, Ryan and Rachel, in 1995.

Cal takes a victory lap around Baltimore's Camden Yards after breaking Lou Gehrig's record of 2,130 consecutive games on September 6, 1995.

Cal fields a grounder during his 2,215th consecutive game in 1996. This game tied the world record for consecutive games held by Sachio Kinugasa of Japan's Hiroshima Carp.

Cal *(second from left)* joins Maryland governor Parris Glendening *(left)*, Aberdeen mayor Doug Wilson *(second from right)*, and his brother Billy for the groundbreaking of Ripken Stadium in 2000.

Cal gives a speech as part of his induction ceremony into the National Baseball Hall of Fame in Cooperstown, New York, in 2007.

News reports stated that the two sides weren't even close to reaching an agreement. The Orioles had reportedly offered a two-year, $10-million deal. Cal and his attorney were asking for a five-year, $39-million contract. The dispute stretched into the season and often overshadowed the on-field action.

Would Cal finally break Gehrig's record in another uniform? The idea seemed unthinkable, even to Cal. He loved Baltimore. He had been an Oriole all his life, and he loved sharing the dugout with his dad and his brother. Cal later admitted that the negotiations were a big distraction to him and may have affected his play. He wasn't hitting well. He couldn't seem to regain the magic he'd had the previous season. His woes were only made worse when he took a Jack Morris pitch to his elbow early in the season, a minor injury that would nag him for weeks.

❝I hear [people] saying I'll never be as good as my brother. Sometimes I want to yell back at them, 'No [kidding].' They think I don't know that?❞

—BILLY RIPKEN

Finally on August 24—Cal's thirty-second birthday—the two sides agreed on an extension. Cal happily signed the five-year,

$30.5-million deal that ensured he'd remain an Oriole through the streak and beyond. The deal brought relief to everyone—the team, Cal, and most of all, the fans.

"I never pictured myself in another uniform," Cal said. "I'm from here. I'm an Oriole, and that's all I ever wanted to be."

Cal's struggles at the plate didn't magically disappear, but the Orioles were winning, and his defensive play was stellar as always. By the end of August, Baltimore was just a half game behind the first-place Blue Jays. In the end, however, they just couldn't keep up with Toronto (which went on to win the World Series). The Orioles finished with a record of 89–73. They had improved on their 1991 total by 22 wins! Still, Cal's offensive numbers—a .251 batting average and just 14 home runs—were a major disappointment. If he'd been able to perform as he had in 1991, there's no telling what the team might have accomplished. Still, the Orioles seemed to be improving, and that was a reason to feel good.

That off-season, however, gave Cal plenty of reasons not to feel good. The Orioles let go of both Billy and Cal Sr., and rumors spread that they'd purposely waited until after Cal signed a contract extension to do it. Cal was hurt. Ever since he had started with the Orioles, he'd shared the dugout with another Ripken. Now Billy was playing for the Texas Rangers, and Rip was watching the games from home.

"I don't know how to put my feelings into words," Cal said. "I'm used to having [my father and brother] here. . . . It feels kind of odd, kind of strange. It hurts me a little bit. . . . In some ways, I [feel] lost out there."

Cal began 1993 the way he had ended 1992: with a slump. Early in the season, his average was a dismal .198. Once again, he tried a new batting stance, standing more upright and not crouching over the plate as much as he had. At first, the new stance showed immediate results. He hit two home runs in his next three games, including a dramatic game winner against the Yankees on May 24. In the end, however, the newfound success didn't last. Once again, Cal slipped back into a slump.

Nothing seemed to be going Cal's way. But that changed on July 26—an off day for the Orioles—when Kelly gave birth to the couple's second child, Ryan Calvin. Cal celebrated the birth by cracking a three-run home run in the following day's game.

Cal and the Orioles managed a winning record in 1993, but their mark of 85–77 was good for just a third-place tie in the division. Cal's numbers were better than the previous season— a .257 average and 24 home runs—but were still a far cry from what he and his fans expected. The MVP season of 1991 already seemed like a distant memory.

Cal, baseball's iron man, made his name by never missing a game. Ironically 1994 was shaping up to be one of the finest seasons of his spectacular career before it was ended early—by a strike. The young season had been full of highlights for Cal. Among them was the 300th home run of his career May 24 against the Brewers. On August 1 against the Twins in Minnesota, he extended his streak to 2,000 games. And most important, he was playing great baseball both in the field and at the plate. His average of .315 and his 13 homers (in 112 games) were more like what he expected of himself. The Orioles were in the playoff hunt, in second place just six games out of first. But all of that came to an end when the players' union and the owners couldn't agree on a new collective bargaining agreement. This agreement defines how players and teams divide baseball's hundreds of millions of dollars in income made during a season.

To the disappointment of players, owners, and especially fans, the players walked out on August 12. At first, few people thought the strike would last long. Games were being canceled, and that cost money for both the players and the owners. But as August dragged on, the two sides couldn't agree on a new deal. Soon Major League Baseball made the shocking announcement that the rest of the season had been canceled—including the playoffs! It would be the first time in ninety years without a World Series. Cal's streak was stuck at 2,009 games—just 122 short of the record.

Bitter negotiations continued throughout the winter. At times the situation seemed hopeless. Neither the players nor the owners were willing to budge. Spring came, and a deal still wasn't in place. The season openers were postponed. The owners talked about using replacement players to start the season. Doing so would have had disastrous results for Cal. His famous streak would end because he would never go against the players' union (even though many fellow players said that he should).

Worse still, Cal's streak became a bargaining chip for the players. The union knew that the owners wanted to see Cal break the record. The Orioles' ownership refused to field replacement players. The city of Baltimore even passed a law to prohibit the use of replacement players at Camden Yards. But in the end, the owners decided against using nonunion players. Finally, in late April 1995, the strike ended. Cal and his fellow players finally got back to work for a shortened (144-game) season.

REALIGNMENT

In 1994 baseball switched from a system of having two divisions in each league to having three—East, Central, and West. All six division champions make the playoffs, as well as one "Wild Card" from each league. (The Wild Card is the team with the best record after the division winners.) The new playoff format was planned for 1994, but because of the strike, it didn't debut until 1995.

When play finally resumed on April 26, 1995, all eyes were on Cal. Bitter feelings still existed between the players and the owners, but they had to work together to win back the loyalty of the millions of baseball fans they had abandoned the year before. They knew that many of the fans wouldn't be quick to forgive the cancellation of the 1994 World Series. But Cal's pursuit of Gehrig's streak would be a big part of rekindling interest in the game. A lot of pressure rested on Cal's shoulders.

"From the first day of spring training in 1995, I realized my life would never be the same again," Cal later wrote. "When I walked onto the field . . . photographers and reporters were everywhere. It was chaos. Bedlam."

The media pressure would only get worse. Everyone wanted to interview Baltimore's Iron Man. He could barely leave his house without being mobbed. The attention was a huge distraction for him, as well as for his teammates. As the season unfolded, Cal and the Orioles would hold an hour-long press conference with each new city the team visited, in hopes that the time spent there would lessen the media's demands. Cal also started staying in a different hotel from the rest of the team, just in hopes he'd be harder to find.

For the loyal Orioles fans, the biggest drama of the season was the question of where Cal would break the record. According to the schedule, he'd reach game number 2,131 on September 6—a game scheduled at Camden Yards against the Angels. But it was the final game of a home stand (a series of games played at a team's home field). A single rainout or other cancellation might result in the record coming on the road. Cal, the Orioles, and his fans all badly wanted the record to come in Baltimore.

A huge reminder of the streak hung on a warehouse across from Camden Yards. The giant sign had a running total of games in Cal's streak. At home games, a new number would be flipped over once the fifth inning was complete. (A game is considered "official" after five innings.) For Oriole fans, the flipping of the numbers was always a reason to cheer, regardless of whether the team was winning or losing.

The season was full of memorable moments for Cal. From his grand slam on June 3 to his diving, game-saving catch on July 6, fans hung on his every move. He was easily the top vote-getter for the All-Star Game, where he went 2 for 3. One of his most surprising memories came on August 9 in New York. Playing in Yankee Stadium—the baseball home of Lou Gehrig and the rival Yankees—he got a standing ovation from Yankee fans, who are famed for being hard on opposing players. In the game, Cal doubled twice, then capped off a great day with an eighth-inning home run into left field. The ball landed near a statue of Lou Gehrig that stands there.

TAKING A TOLL

The weeks leading up to the record were tough on Cal. "I've been very achy the last few weeks," he said. "Maybe it's nerves. It's been a difficult time. It's been tough to sleep. Usually I sleep like a rock. But there's a switch in my body that won't turn off. I toss and turn. It's been exhausting."

Cal received other standing ovations as he drew closer to the record. Wherever he went, he was met with cheers. Even entire opposing teams saluted Cal. At the end of game number 2,128 (three from the record), the Seattle Mariners stood on the edge of the dugout and applauded. The Angels came to Baltimore next and did the same. "Every one of the Angels wanted to run over and give Cal a high five," said Angel infielder Rex Hudler.

On September 5, Cal took the field for the record-tying game, number 2,130. The Orioles weren't in a pennant race (they'd hung tough through late July, then had faded out of contention in August), but the fans scarcely noticed. Tickets were nearly impossible to buy. The packed stadium erupted when outfielder Brady Anderson caught a fly ball to end the top of the fifth inning. The Orioles were ahead 7–0. The number on the warehouse changed. (If the game had been tied or the Orioles were behind after the top of the fifth inning, the teams would have needed to play the rest of the inning before the game was official.) For that one day, Cal and Gehrig stood together atop the list.

The crowd wouldn't stop going nuts. After a long delay, the game finally resumed. Cal stepped to the plate in the bottom of the inning, facing Angel pitcher Tom Holzemer, who threw him a slider (a type of curveball). Cal took a healthy cut—*CRACK!* The ball sailed in a high arc and barely cleared the left-field fence for a home run. The Oriole fans, who had never really stopped cheering, roared all the louder. It was a gratifying moment for Cal. The eyes of the baseball world were on him, and he desperately wanted to play well. What could be more memorable than cranking a homer in the very same inning that he tied the record? The Orioles were pumped up and went on to win the game 8–0. The stage was set for the big day—game 2,131.

Camden Yards was packed on September 6. More than 750 media members were on hand for the game. Cal and the Orioles set aside 260 special seats, each of which sold for $5,000. The money raised went to research for ALS (the disease that killed Gehrig).

Before the game, Cal was understandably nervous. In the clubhouse, he met President Bill Clinton and Vice President Al Gore. Cal later admitted that he was sweating heavily during the meeting and that he didn't stop sweating most of that night.

In the fourth inning, Cal came to the plate with the Orioles clinging to a 2–1 lead. Angel pitcher Shawn Boskie fell behind in the count at 3 balls, no strikes. Cal would normally take a pitch in that situation, in hopes of drawing a walk. But not that night. Too many people had come just to see him play on his big day. When he saw Boskie's fastball coming right down the center of the strike zone, he swung. The previous night, his home run had barely cleared the fence. He hadn't even known it was going out when he hit it. But this night, there was no doubt. As soon as he made contact, he knew. The ball sailed high and far for yet another home run. The ovation was deafening. The people had come to see Cal play, and he hadn't disappointed them.

The next inning brought the moment Cal, his teammates, and baseball fans around the world had been waiting for. When second baseman Manny Alexander caught the final out of the top of the fifth inning, the game—and Cal's record—were official. The number on the huge banner dropped to 2,131. The crowd was electric. The celebration was on.

Cal looked up into the stands and found his parents. He walked over to where Kelly and the kids were sitting. He picked up Ryan and gave Rachel a kiss. Then he headed back to the dugout, thinking that would be the end of it. He knew the Orioles would hold a postgame ceremony later. But for now, he thought, it was time to get back to baseball.

The fans had other ideas. The stadium thundered with applause. It just kept going and going. Cal's teammate Rafael Palmeiro finally told him, "You're going to have to take a lap [around the stadium]. That's the only way they'll quit."

Cal didn't want to do it. He wanted to get back to baseball and save the celebration for later. But after another ten minutes, he realized that Palmeiro was right. The fans weren't going to stop until he came out and shared the moment with them. He started out tentatively, but soon the emotion took over. He ran around the perimeter of the field, shaking hands, smiling, and giving high fives. Finally, after a twenty-two-minute delay, the game got back under way. The Orioles held on to the lead Cal had helped to build, winning the game 4–2. And then another celebration began—the on-field ceremony to honor Cal.

Cal's speech was the highlight of the ceremony. He thanked his family, as well as his teammates and coaches of past and present. Then he spoke about his link with Gehrig. "Some may think our greatest connection is that we both played many consecutive games," he said. "Yet I believe in my heart that the true link is the common motivation of a love of the game of baseball, a passion for your team, and a desire to compete at the very highest level. I know that if Lou Gehrig is looking down on tonight's activities, he isn't concerned with someone's playing more games than he did. Instead, he's viewing tonight as just another example of what's good and right about the great American game. . . . You are challenged by the game of baseball to do your very best, day in and day out, and that's all I've ever tried to do."

Chapter Eight

The Late Innings

Cal's streak didn't stop at 2,131. To the surprise of no one, he played in the rest of Baltimore's games in 1995, finishing the season with a batting average of .262 and 17 home runs. During the off-season, *Sports Illustrated* and *Sporting News* each named him Sportsman of the Year. The Associated Press, meanwhile, named him Male Athlete of the Year.

And in 1996, the streak just kept going. With the worst of the media attention gone, Cal and his teammates could concentrate on a more important goal—returning to the playoffs. The powerful Baltimore lineup gave Cal his best chance yet to reach the postseason for the first time since his second full season. The Orioles were winning under new manager Davey Johnson, and Cal was a big part of the success. On May 28, he did something he'd never done in the big leagues before—he launched three home runs in the same game. The third homer was the

333rd of his career, tying him with Murray for the all-time Oriole record. Meanwhile the Orioles and the Yankees were battling for the AL East lead.

Billy briefly returned to the Orioles for the 1996 season. He played in only 57 games, however, and struggled to a .230 batting average.

Johnson was also experimenting with moving Cal to third base. Cal still played shortstop most of the time, but he also started some games at third base. While many fans objected and even Cal himself wasn't sure of the move, Johnson felt sure that Cal would end his career where he had started it.

With the way the Orioles were playing, no one could question Johnson's decisions too much. The AL East race remained hot for most of the summer, as did Cal's bat. He was once again voted the AL starting shortstop in the All-Star Game. Ironically, Cal's streak almost ended at the All-Star festivities, though not during the game. During photographs, White Sox pitcher Roberto Hernandez slipped and flailed his arms out to catch his balance. His elbow cracked Cal right in the nose, breaking it. But Cal—tough as nails—didn't miss a single game, not even the All-Star Game. Those who knew him weren't even a little bit surprised.

On June 14, 1996, Cal played in his 2,215th-straight game, surpassing the mark of Sachio Kinugasa, who had played baseball in Japan.

The Yankees slowly pulled away from the Orioles, building a nearly insurmountable ten-game lead. In past years, Baltimore would have been out of luck. But with the addition of the Wild Card, the Orioles were still able to fight for a playoff spot. The team traded for Eddie Murray to help with the stretch run. Cal was thrilled to have his old teammate and friend back with the team, and the move paid off on the field. Cal, Murray, and the Orioles finished the season at 88–74, good enough to qualify for the playoffs as the Wild Card—the Orioles' first postseason appearance in thirteen years! The Orioles also set a major league record with 257 home runs in the regular season. Cal's .278 batting average and 26 home runs had marked yet another revival in his long, up-and-down career.

Waiting for Cal and the Orioles were the Cleveland Indians. Cleveland, the Central Division champion, was heavily favored in the best-of-five series. They had put up an impressive 99–62 record during the season and were a year removed from playing in the World Series. Meanwhile, the Baltimore roster was filled with players who had little or no playoff experience—even Cal had played in just one postseason.

Still, the Orioles were undaunted. In the first game, they exploded for ten runs, including a third-inning RBI single from Cal. Baltimore easily took the game 10–4. The Baltimore bats were at it again in game two. Cal had a single in a three-run fifth inning that propelled Baltimore to a 7–4 win and a two-game edge in the series. They had to win just one of the remaining three games to advance to the ALCS.

The Indians stormed back to take game three, then set their sights at evening the series and forcing a winner-take-all finale. And for a while, it looked like that's exactly what would happen. The Indians took a 3–2 lead into the ninth inning of game four, but with the Orioles down to their final out, second baseman Robbie Alomar hit a light RBI single to tie it up. Extra innings! The game dragged on. The tenth and eleventh innings passed with the teams deadlocked. Everyone in the stadium could feel the tension. Finally, in the twelfth inning, Alomar's home run made him the hero once again. The Orioles had done it! They'd knocked off the Indians three games to one and were headed to the ALCS to face the Yankees! Cal, who had batted

.444 with three doubles in the four games, celebrated the win with his teammates.

Game one of the ALCS, played at Yankee Stadium, was a game few Oriole fans will ever forget. It was a tight contest, with the Orioles clinging to a 4–3 lead in the bottom of the eighth inning. With one out, Yankee shortstop Derek Jeter stepped to the plate. Jeter hit a fly ball to deep right field. Baltimore outfielder Tony Tarasco chased the ball to the warning track and positioned himself to make a play. But just as the ball was coming down, a young Yankee fan named Jeffrey Maier reached over the railing and tried to catch the ball, deflecting it into the stands. By baseball rules, a fan cannot touch a ball in the field of play. The umpires should have called interference and either called Jeter out or awarded him a double. But they blew the call and gave Jeter a game-tying home run. The game went into extra innings, the Yankees won, and Jeffrey Maier became a hero in New York and a villain in Baltimore.

The Orioles briefly recovered, winning game two to tie the best-of-seven series at one game apiece. For the next three games, the teams traveled to Baltimore's Camden Yards. In game three, despite scoring two runs in the bottom of the first inning, the Orioles lost 5–2. The following day, the Orioles had another promising start, but they lost 8–4. Game five was Baltimore's last chance. Another New York win would send the Yankees to the

World Series. In the third inning, the Yankees scored six runs, and it was all but over for the Orioles. Even three Baltimore home runs later in the game weren't enough—they lost game five 6–4.

Baltimore's season was over. But after years of futility, Cal, his teammates, and his fans finally had a reason to be optimistic. The team had enjoyed a great year in 1996, and 1997 was shaping up to be even better.

 In 1997 Cal published his autobiography, *The Only Way I Know*.

The inevitable finally happened in 1997—Cal made the switch full-time to third base. He'd never been known as quick, and by age thirty-six, he had lost much of what quickness he'd had. So when Baltimore acquired a young shortstop named Mike Bordick, Cal was ready to make the move. He knew that it was best for the team.

The Orioles followed up their success in 1996 with an even better 1997. They won their first game and never looked back, leading the AL East for the entire season. Cal was putting up great offensive numbers before a back injury started to hamper his production. The injury affected Cal's performance so much that many fans were calling for him to take a well-earned rest. After all, he already had Gehrig's record, so why not get healthy for the playoffs? But Cal wouldn't hear of sitting. The streak lived on, even if Cal wasn't able to maintain his early-season success. Despite the injury, Cal's final numbers were respectable—a .270 average with 17 home runs. More important, the Orioles enjoyed a 98–64 season and won the AL East. For the second year in a row, it was playoff time!

Baltimore faced the Seattle Mariners in the opening round. The heavily favored Orioles had no trouble knocking out Seattle, opening the series with a pair of 9–3 wins, then closing out the Mariners in four games. Cal proved that his back wasn't slowing him down too much, batting .438 in the series.

---

66 *[Cal is] an amazing guy. Sure, he's stubborn. But that's what makes him great. He will not accept failure. It's what has made him a great player all these years. He's an uncompromising guy.* **99**

—BALTIMORE HITTING COACH RICK DOWN

The Indians waited in the ALCS. The Orioles were favored to advance to the World Series, and they won the opener 3–0. But from that moment, nothing seemed to go right for the team. In game two, Cal's two-run homer in the second inning helped push the Orioles to an early 4–2 lead. But Baltimore's bullpen couldn't hold the lead, giving up three eighth-inning runs and allowing Cleveland to even the series at a game apiece.

In game three, a bizarre play in extra innings gave the Indians a 2–1 series lead. Cleveland shortstop Omar Vizquel tried to bunt with a runner at third base. The Orioles thought that Vizquel's bat tipped the pitch foul. The ball rolled away from Oriole catcher Lenny Webster. But the umpire ruled that Vizquel's bat had never touched it, meaning that the ball was live and in play. The runner at third dashed home, and none of the confused Orioles even tried to stop the winning run from scoring. It was a bitterly disappointing way to lose such an important game.

The strangeness continued in game four, when another unlikely play contributed to an 8–7 Cleveland victory. This time a wild pitch from Oriole reliever Arthur Rhodes allowed two runs to score. The umpire accidentally got in Webster's way, blocking his view of the ball. Two runs came around to score before Webster recovered and found the ball. The Orioles found themselves trailing 3–1 in the series, and they couldn't seem to catch a break.

Baltimore came back to win game five, but Cleveland took game six in extra innings to complete the upset. And once again Oriole fans were in a state of disbelief. The final called strike that ended the series—on Roberto Alomar—

appeared to be inside, out of the strike zone. But arguing would do the team no good. After a brilliant regular season, the playoffs ended for the Orioles. In the championship series, Cal batted .348 with one homer. It would be the last playoff series of his amazing career.

For Cal Ripken fans, 1998 will always be remembered as the year that his consecutive games streak finally ended. The Orioles couldn't reproduce their success of 1997, and Cal's power numbers were way down. By September, Cal knew that it was time for the streak to end. His manager, Ray Miller, wasn't about to be the man who ended it, though. So on September 20, Cal did it himself. "I think the time is right," he told Miller.

At first, when young Ryan Minor took the field at third base, few fans at Camden Yards understood what was happening—there had been no announcement about Cal's decision. But after the game's first out, the visiting Yankees stood on the edge of their dugout to salute Cal with a standing ovation. The fans soon caught on and followed suit. Cal had to come out of the Baltimore dugout twice to tip his cap before the game resumed. Nine innings later, his amazing streak officially ended at 2,632.

"I guess I just want to say it was time," Cal said in a news conference after the game. "Baseball has always been a team game, and I've always thought that the focus should be on the team. And there have been times . . . that the focus was on the streak and I never felt totally comfortable about that. It just reached a point where I firmly believe that it was time to change the subject and restore the focus back to where it should be and move on."

In 1998 Cal played in 161 of his team's 162 games. He batted .271 with 14 home runs.

 Cal's father died of lung cancer in 1999, two weeks before opening day.

The next two seasons of Cal's career bore little resemblance to the first eighteen. After going almost two decades without any major injuries, Cal's aching back finally forced him to the sidelines. He played in just 86 games in 1999. After several trips to the disabled list, back surgery finally ended his season in September. Even though he'd played in only a little more than half of Baltimore's games, it had been a brilliant season for Cal, who batted a career-high .340 with 18 home runs. If he'd maintained that pace for an entire season, it would have been the best of his career. His season highlight came on June 13 against the Atlanta Braves. In the game, Cal went 6 for 6 with 2 homers (becoming the first Oriole to amass 6 hits in a single game). Another big moment came on September 2, when he smacked the 400th home run of his career.

As he had in 1999, Cal played only about half of the team's games in 2000. Once again his back forced him to miss time. He later admitted that he'd tried to come back from his 1999 surgery too quickly. But that didn't stop him from achieving one of baseball's most hallowed milestones—3,000 career hits—on April 15. The milestone came in Minnesota against the Twins. Facing Hector Carrasco, Cal stroked a solid single up the middle. At first base, he met his friend Oriole first-base coach Eddie Murray. "Way to go, welcome to the club," said Murray, who had also gotten his 3,000th hit in Minnesota.

ELITE COMPANY

When Cal got hit number 3,000, he became only the seventh player in major league history to amass 400 career homers and 3,000 career hits. The six who did it before him were Hank Aaron, Willie Mays, Eddie Murray, Stan Musial, Dave Winfield, and Carl Yastrzemski.

Put together, Cal's 1999 and 2000 totaled about one full season's worth of games. Combined, they would have added up to one of his finest seasons—a .300 average, 33 homers, and 113 RBI in 169 games.

"At the end [of the 2000 season] I was coming off a period of time when I was out, when I blew my back out again, and if I lump those two years together, they were a struggle physically," he said. Cal wasn't ready to make an announcement, but he had already started to realize that the 2001 season would be his last.

Chapter Nine

Hanging It Up

The 2001 season was both a long celebration of Cal's amazing career and a bittersweet end filled with struggles. If any doubts about retirement had entered into Cal's mind, the first half of 2001 quickly changed them. Once again the Orioles were struggling. The team had gotten worse every season since their fabulous 1997, and Cal was battling both nagging injuries and a terrible slump. When he made his formal retirement announcement in mid-June, he was batting a lowly .210. Observers pointed out that the bat speed of the forty-year-old infielder had slowed considerably. He had to "cheat" on pitches by starting his swing a fraction of a second earlier, which gave him that much less time to judge the pitch's speed and location. Age had finally caught up with Cal.

As soon as he announced that he would be retiring, the season became an extended farewell tour. In every city, the fans gave him a standing ovation. They didn't care that he was no longer the old reliable Cal who was in the lineup producing every day. His aches and pains, along with his struggles, had turned him into a part-time player. But even that didn't stop the fans from electing him to start in one last All-Star Game that July.

STAYING ON THE FIELD

Many older players prolong their careers by playing as the designated hitter (DH). But Cal didn't want that. After all, his career had centered around him playing in the field every day. In his career, Cal played just 24 games at DH—all of them in his final two injury-plagued seasons.

Cal soaked in the All-Star experience. He was the first player in the American League clubhouse, not wanting to miss a moment. Before the game, ceremonies honored both Cal and Tony Gwynn, another longtime star who had announced his retirement. When the game started, Cal trotted out of the dugout to take his position at third base. But Texas's Alex Rodriguez, elected by the fans to start at shortstop, wouldn't let Cal take that position. With a smile, Rodriguez pointed Cal to the shortstop position before walking to third base himself. Cal was one of Rodriguez's heroes, and the star slugger wanted to see him play shortstop one last time. It was an emotional moment for both players as well as everyone else at Seattle's Safeco Field.

❝*[Switching positions] was an opportunity to let everybody reminisce about what a great career [Cal] had as a shortstop.*❞

—ALEX RODRIGUEZ ON SWITCHING POSITIONS
WITH CAL RIPKEN IN THE 2001 ALL-STAR GAME

"At that point, fear ran through my veins," Cal later said. "I thought, the world stage wasn't the time to go back to short-stop. But as I thought more, I thought it was a great tribute."

It was just the beginning of a memorable night. In the third inning, Cal stepped to the plate against Chan Ho Park of the Los Angeles Dodgers to yet another ovation. Cal raised his arm to the crowd, then stepped up to the plate. Park's first pitch was a fast-ball on the inside half of the plate. Cal took a big swing and hit it solidly. Cameras all around the stadium flashed as the ball sailed over the left-field fence for a home run. The applause was deaf-ening as Cal rounded the bases and headed back to the dugout, and it didn't stop until he came out to tip his hat to the fans.

"I felt like I was flying around the bases," Cal said. "It was a shot of adrenaline, and then the curtain call after that; it was just a continuation of those goose bumps. I still have them right now, thinking about it. When you have the chance, just one opportunity in front of a big baseball crowd and feel the moment, feel the electricity, the magic from the moment, that's everything."

The homer propelled the American League to a 4–1 victory, and to the surprise of no one, Cal was named MVP of the game. He became the first American League player ever to win the award more than once and did so exactly ten years after his memorable performance in the 1991 All-Star Game.

The high of the All-Star festivities marked a brief revival for Cal, who got hot after the break. At one point, he got a hit in 16 consecutive games, and by late August his batting average was up to .277. Cal enjoyed every moment, spending all the time he could at the ballpark, signing extra autographs for fans, and just enjoying the experience.

"I come into ballparks with my eyes open a little wider," he said of his farewell tour. "I try to take in all the things that maybe you take for granted that are pretty special moments. They could be dumb things like sitting on the bench by yourself and looking out over Fenway [Park]. There's a certain peace and feeling you have looking out on the field. Or it could be sitting in the clubhouse with a couple of guys."

But the tour was quickly winding down. On September 23, Cal's home run against the Yankees was his last. Perhaps the pressure or the emotion got to Cal in those final weeks of 2001. Or maybe it was nothing more than exhaustion. Whatever the reason, Cal ended his career in one of his worst slumps, collecting just 2 hits in his final 48 at bats.

The Red Sox were in Baltimore for Cal's final game on October 6. Originally, the Orioles were scheduled to finish their season in New York, but the terrorist attacks of September 11 forced the league to shuffle the late-season schedules. A reporter asked Cal if he was sad to see his long career ending. The forty-one-year-old was not. "I've had my fill," he answered. He was ready.

❝I think [Cal is] one of the few players in the history of any sport that doesn't have any regrets as he leaves the game. His is a retirement like no other in the history of baseball, I'd imagine.❞

—BALTIMORE OUTFIELDER BRADY ANDERSON

The pregame ceremony honoring Cal was filled with surprises. The Orioles presented him with a beautiful vase with images of both Memorial Stadium and Camden Yards. They gave him a $1-million check for the Aberdeen Project, a drive he had started to build a stadium and baseball academy in his hometown of Aberdeen. Then Oriole owner Peter Angelos and his wife, Georgia, presented Cal with a beautiful portrait of Cal Sr. Remembering his father and looking at the portrait, Cal later said, was the most powerful moment of the night.

But there was more. The honors kept coming, from video highlights to words from former president Clinton. Baltimore mayor Martin O'Malley announced that the city had renamed a street Ripken Way. Baseball commissioner Bud Selig unveiled a new award—the Cal Ripken Jr. Award—that would be presented to any player who appeared in all of his team's games for a season. And the Orioles retired Cal's number 8 jersey. No one on the team would ever wear that number again.

Finally, it was time to take the field. But the Orioles had one more surprise for Cal. When he took his spot at third base, he wasn't looking out at his fellow 2001 Orioles teammates. Instead, standing at each of the other positions were the players from Cal's first major league start—Murray, Singleton, McGregor, and the rest. Even Earl Weaver was there standing in foul territory. Only the shortstop position was empty, in tribute to Mark Belanger, who died of lung cancer in 1998.

When the current Oriole players took the field, the game itself didn't offer any highlights. Those hoping to see Cal get one last home run, hit, or even an Orioles victory didn't get their wish. Cal was left standing in the on-deck circle when Brady Anderson struck out to end the game. Despite the thunderous chant of "We want Cal," it was over.

The Orioles had lost their 98th game of a long season, but still the fans remained cheering. Cal came back out onto the field one last time to thank his fans. "One question I've been repeatedly asked these last few weeks is how do I want to be remembered. My answer has been simple: To be remembered at all is pretty special."

Cal stepped off the field, and for the first time in forty-five years, the Orioles organization was without a Ripken. Players on the 2002 team would comment on how empty Cal's corner of the clubhouse felt. New players would ask which locker had been Cal's. Even though he was no longer with the team, his legacy remained.

Cal and Billy briefly hosted a satellite-radio talk show. They talked about baseball, from Little League to the big leagues.

For his part, Cal was ready to move on to the next phase of his life. He was excited about the chance to spend more time with his loved ones as well as to pursue new dreams. Through the Aberdeen Project, he was able to build a stadium in his hometown. He and Billy also started the Cal Ripken Sr. Foundation, which gives underprivileged children the chance to attend a baseball camp. Cal even started his own baseball academy in Myrtle Beach, South Carolina. And he also followed another dream of helping to run a baseball team by buying several minor-league teams, including the Aberdeen Ironbirds, a team that plays in the stadium Cal helped to build. He was even rumored to be part of a group seeking to purchase the Orioles.

"I think I could have value to [an ownership group]," he said in 2005, when the rumors were at their peak. "I like [Peter] Angelos, and I don't know what's going to happen with the club, but if it were for sale, it would be interesting to anyone."

In August 2007, U.S. Secretary of State Condoleezza Rice named Cal a goodwill ambassador. Cal's job is to help improve the worldwide image of the United States through baseball. Cal was excited about the new role and immediately began planning a trip to China.

Writing has become another of Cal's passions. He has authored several books on his life as well as his approach to baseball, competition, and even parenting. He has written advice columns for the *Baltimore Sun* newspaper. And if all of that isn't enough, Cal has also helped to produce his own series of baseball training videos.

In many ways, Cal remained in the spotlight long after his retirement. That was never more true than in 2007, when he received baseball's highest honor—election into the Hall of Fame—in his first year of eligibility. Players must be retired for five years before they can be enshrined. Cal received 537 out of 545 votes—the third-highest percentage in Hall of Fame voting history.

In 2007 another Baltimore shortstop had a consecutive games streak end. Miguel Tejada's streak of 1,152 straight games ended when a pitch hit and broke his wrist.

About 70,000 fans flocked to Cooperstown, New York, on July 29 to see Cal and Gwynn be inducted into baseball's Hall of Fame. In his acceptance speech, Cal was uncharacteristically emotional. He choked up as he talked about his dad and his family. He thanked his teammates and the fans.

He concluded, "I truly believe there are no endings, just points at which we begin again, as players do 162 times a season and if they are lucky, a few more times each fall. And finally, I can only hope that all of us, whether we have played on the field or been fans in the stands, can reflect on how fortunate we are and can see our lives as new beginnings that allow us to leave this world a bit better than when we came into it."

Epilogue

Cal's Legacy

In an era where few ballplayers remain with the same team for an entire career, Cal was a true rarity. He wasn't just an Oriole for twenty-one years either. He'd been an Oriole from the day he was born. Despite his amazing statistics and his famous streak, that may be Cal's most amazing legacy. He could have had even more fame and playoff glory in a Yankee or Red Sox uniform. But Cal was an Oriole, as loyal as any player can be, even through some long, dark stretches of losing season after losing season.

Cal was the model of consistency. He had 3,184 career hits but only twice did he get more than 200 in a season. He had 431 career home runs but hit more than 30 only once. Cal just showed up every day and did his job. He didn't make his mark by being spectacular; he made it by being reliable. A manager knew just what he was getting out of number 8—hard work, dedication, and a love of the game.

For baseball fans, it's impossible to separate Cal from the streak. When he was elected to the Hall of Fame on the first ballot, many wondered how heavily the streak weighed into the voting. After all, with two AL MVP trophies, a World Series title, and a pile of personal milestones, Cal's numbers were enough to earn his ticket to the Hall even if the streak had never happened. But the streak did happen, and it changed the way fans looked at the game and the men who play it. Cal was a boy who grew up on baseball diamonds, watching, learning, and living the game every day. It should come as little surprise that we would remember him for doing exactly that.

PERSONAL STATISTICS

Name:
Calvin Edwin Ripken Jr.

Nicknames:
Iron Man

Born:
August 24, 1960

Height:
6' 4"

Weight:
225 lbs.

Throws:
Right-handed

Bats:
Right-handed

BATTING STATISTICS

Year	Team	Avg	G	AB	Runs	Hits	2B	3B	HR	RBI	SB
1981	Orioles	0.128	23	39	1	5	0	0	0	0	0
1982	Orioles	0.264	160	598	90	158	32	5	28	93	3
1983	Orioles	0.318	162	663	121	211	47	2	27	102	0
1984	Orioles	0.304	162	641	103	195	37	7	27	86	2
1985	Orioles	0.282	161	642	116	181	32	5	26	110	2
1986	Orioles	0.282	162	627	98	177	35	1	25	81	4
1987	Orioles	0.252	162	624	97	157	28	3	27	98	3
1988	Orioles	0.264	161	575	87	152	25	1	23	81	2
1989	Orioles	0.257	162	646	80	166	30	0	21	93	3
1990	Orioles	0.250	161	600	78	150	28	4	21	84	3
1991	Orioles	0.323	162	650	99	210	46	5	34	114	6
1992	Orioles	0.251	162	637	73	160	29	1	14	72	4
1993	Orioles	0.257	162	641	87	165	26	3	24	90	1
1994	Orioles	0.315	112	444	71	140	19	3	13	75	1
1995	Orioles	0.262	144	550	71	144	33	2	17	88	0
1996	Orioles	0.278	163	640	94	178	40	1	26	102	1
1997	Orioles	0.270	162	615	79	166	30	0	17	84	1
1998	Orioles	0.271	161	601	65	163	27	1	14	61	0

BATTING STATISTICS (continued)

Year	Team	Avg	G	AB	Runs	Hits	2B	3B	HR	RBI	SB
1999	Orioles	0.340	86	332	51	113	27	0	18	57	0
2000	Orioles	0.256	83	309	43	79	16	0	15	56	0
2001	Orioles	0.239	128	477	43	114	16	0	14	68	0
	Totals:	0.276	3,001	11,551	1,647	3,184	603	44	431	1,695	36

Key: **Avg**: batting average; **G**: games; **AB**: at bats; **2B**: doubles; **3B**: triples; **HR**: home runs; **RBI**: runs batted in; **SB**: stolen bases

FIELDING STATISTICS

Year	Team	Pos	G	C	PO	A	E	DP	FLD%
1981	BAL	SS	12	37	11	24	2	5	0.946
		3B	6	9	2	6	1	1	0.889
1982	BAL	SS	94	457	155	289	13	47	0.972
		3B	71	223	66	151	6	17	0.973
1983	BAL	SS	162	831	272	534	25	113	0.970
1984	BAL	SS	162	906	297	583	26	122	0.971
1985	BAL	SS	161	786	286	474	26	123	0.967
1986	BAL	SS	162	735	240	482	13	105	0.982
1987	BAL	SS	162	740	240	480	20	103	0.973
1988	BAL	SS	161	785	284	480	21	119	0.973
1989	BAL	SS	162	815	276	531	8	119	0.990
1990	BAL	SS	161	680	242	435	3	94	0.996
1991	BAL	SS	162	806	267	528	11	114	0.986
1992	BAL	SS	162	744	287	445	12	119	0.984
1993	BAL	SS	162	738	226	495	17	101	0.977
1994	BAL	SS	112	460	132	321	7	72	0.985
1995	BAL	SS	144	622	206	409	7	100	0.989
1996	BAL	SS	158	709	228	467	14	109	0.980
		3B	6	21	5	16	0	1	1.000
1997	BAL	SS	3	2	2	0	0	0	1.000

FIELDING STATISTICS (continued)

Year	Team	Pos	G	C	PO	A	E	DP	FLD%
		3B	162	434	98	314	22	25	0.949
1998	BAL	3B	161	374	101	265	8	22	0.979
1999	BAL	3B	85	191	36	142	13	11	0.932
2000	BAL	3B	73	195	56	134	5	17	0.974
		DH	10						
2001	BAL	3B	111	320	97	209	14	23	0.956
		DH	14						
	Total		3,001	12,620	4,112	8,214	294	1,682	0.977

Key: Pos: position; G: games; C: chances (balls hit to a position); PO: putouts; A: assists; E: errors;
DP: double plays; FLD%: fielding percentage

GLOSSARY

amyotrophic lateral sclerosis (ALS): a disease that causes a person's nerves to deteriorate. It's also called Lou Gehrig's disease.

autobiography: a book written about a person's own life

collective bargaining agreement: an agreement between owners and players that covers all aspects of the players' employment, from working conditions to pay and benefits

draft: a system for selecting new players for professional sports teams

free agent: a player who isn't currently under a contract and is free to sign with any team

rookie: a first-year player

slump: a prolonged period in which an athlete performs far below his or her normal level

strike: a walkout by a group of workers. Workers strike in an attempt to get higher wages, better working conditions, or more benefits.

wild card: the best non-division-winning team in each league

SOURCES

3 Cal Ripken Jr. and Mike Bryan, *The Only Way I Know* (New York: Viking, 1997), 202.

4 Harvey Rosenfeld, *Iron Man: The Cal Ripken Jr. Story* (New York: St. Martin's Press, 1995), 183.

7 Rosenfeld, *Iron Man*, 2.

7 Jim Campbell, *Cal Ripken Jr.* (Philadelphia: Chelsea House Publishers, 1997), 21.

8 Rosenfeld, *Iron Man*, 4.

9 Ripken, *The Only Way I Know*, 11.

10 Rosenfeld, *Iron Man*, 9.

10 Ibid., 2.

14 Ibid., 17.

15 Lois Nicholson, *Cal Ripken Jr.: Quiet Hero*, (Centreville, MD: Tidewater Publishers, 1995), 37.

26 Rosenfeld, *Iron Man*, 27.

21 Ibid., 53.

21 Nicholson, *Cal Ripken Jr.: Quiet Hero*, 51.

23 Cal Ripken Jr. and Mike Bryan, *Cal Ripken, Jr.: My Story*, Adapted by Dan Gutman from *The Only Way I Know*, (New York: Dial Books for Young Readers, 1999), 29.

23 Rosenfeld, *Iron Man*, 62.

23 Ripken, *The Only Way I Know*, 85.

27 Rosenfeld, *Iron Man*, 73.

27 Ibid., 88.

28 Nicholson, *Cal Ripken Jr.: Quiet Hero*, 60.

28 Rosenfeld, *Iron Man*, 79.

29 Ibid., 84.

30 Baltimore Sun Staff, "Q&A: Being Elected . . . It's the Ultimate," *Baltimore Sun*, January 10, 2007, www.baltimoresun.com/sports/baseball/ripken/bal-sp.ripkenqa10jan10,0,3953173.story?coll=bal-sports-ripken (December 28, 2007).

32 Rosenfeld, *Iron Man*, 88.

33–34 Ibid., 61.

34 Snyder, Brad, "Out One Era, into Another," *Baltimore Sun*, September 23, 1999, www.baltimoresun.com/sports/

baseball/ripken/bal-cal1984sep23,0,1072933.htmlstory (December 28, 2007).

34 Rosenfeld, *Iron Man*, 98.

36 Snyder, Brad, "Fred Lynn, a Healthy Respect," *Baltimore Sun*, September 23, 1999, www.baltimoresun.com/sports/baseball/ripken/bal-cal1985sep23,0,1466150.htmlstory (December 28, 2007).

37 Rosenfeld, *Iron Man*, 100.

38 Ripken, *The Only Way I Know*, 147.

38 Nicholson, *Cal Ripken Jr.: Quiet Hero*, 69.

40 Rosenfeld, *Iron Man*, 120.

41 Ibid., 128.

42 Nicholson, *Cal Ripken Jr.: Quiet Hero*, 72.

43 Rosenfield, *Iron Man*, 130.

44 Ripken, *Cal Ripken, Jr.: My Story*, 58.

45 Rosenfield, *Iron Man*, 144.

46 Ibid., 146.

49 Snyder, Brad, "Back into Winning Swing," *Baltimore Sun*, September 23, 1999, www.baltimoresun.com/sports/baseball/ripken/bal-cal1989sep23,0,3039018.htmlstory (December 28, 2007).

53 Rosenfeld, *Iron Man*, 183.

52 Ibid., 164.

53 Ibid., 167.

54 Ibid., 178.

57 Ibid., 189.

59 Ibid., 219.

60 Ibid., 207.

61 Ibid., 221.

64 Ripken, *Cal Ripken, Jr.: My Story*, 88.

66 Campbell, *Cal Ripken Jr.*, 9.

66 Ibid., 53.

68 Ibid., 15.

69 Ripken, *The Only Way I Know*, 307.

70 Ibid., 311.

77 *Baltimore Sun*, "After 2,632 Consecutive Games, Iron Man Takes a Seat," September 23, 1999, www.baltimoresun.com/sports/baseball/ripken/bal-cal1998sep23,0,3104554.htmlstory (December 28, 2007).

79 Associated Press, "I Think the Time Is Right," *CNNsi.com*, September 20, 1998, http://sportsillustrated.cnn.com/baseball/mlb/news/1998/09/20/ripken_streak/ (December 28, 2007).

80 *Baltimore Sun*, "After 2,632 Consecutive Games, Iron Man Takes a Seat."

81 Antonen, Mel, "Ripken Connects for 3,000th hit," *USA Today*, April 17, 2000.

82 Jeff Seidel, *Baseball's Iron Man: Cal Ripken Jr.* (Champaign, IL: Sports Publishing, 2007), 58.

85 John Hickey, "Cal's Curtain Call Ripken Blasts Homer, Earns All-Star MVP," *Seattle Post-Intelligencer*, July 11,2001, D1.

85 Andriesen, David, "Cal Goes Out with a Bang," *Seattle Post-Intelligencer*, July 11, 2001, http://seattlepi.nwsource.com/baseball/30846_mvp11.shtml (December 28, 2007).

86 Ibid.

86 *Cal: Celebrating the Career of a Baseball Legend* (St. Louis: Sporting News; Baltimore: Baltimore Sun Co., 2001), 43.

87 "Baseball's Iron Man: 'I've had 20 full years . . .'," *ABC News*, September 30, 2004, http://abcnews.go.com/Sports/story?id=997 11&page=1 (December 28, 2007).

87 Eisenberg, John, "In Ripken's Sentimental Journey, Last Chance to Play Is the Real Trip," *Baltimore Sun*. October 7, 2001, www.baltimoresun.com/sports/baseball/ripken/bal-sp.eisenberg07oct07,0,4148660.column?coll=bal-utility-ripken (December 28, 2007).

89 *Cal: Celebrating the Career of a Baseball Legend*, 35.

90 Seidel, *Baseball's Iron Man*, xvi.

92 Ripken speech 7-29-07.txt, Baseball Hall of Fame, July 29, 2007, http://web.baseballhalloffame.org/news/download/ripken_speech.pdf (December 28, 2007).

BIBLIOGRAPHY

Campbell, Jim. *Cal Ripken Jr.* Philadelphia: Chelsea House
  Publishers, 1997.

Nicholson, Lois. *Cal Ripken Jr.: Quiet Hero.* Centreville, MD:
  Tidewater Publishers, 1995.

Ripken, Cal, Jr., and Mike Bryan. *The Only Way I Know.* New
  York: Viking, 1997.

Ripken, Cal, Jr., and Mike Bryan. *Cal Ripken, Jr.: My Story.*
  Adapted by Dan Gutman from *The Only Way I Know.* New
  York; Dial Books for Young Readers, 1999.

Rosenfeld, Harvey. *Iron Man: The Cal Ripken Jr. Story.* New
  York: St. Martin's Press, 1995.

Seidel, Jeff. *Baseball's Iron Man: Cal Ripken Jr.* Champaign, IL:
  Sports Publishing, 2007.

Sporting News. *Cal: Celebrating the Career of a Baseball Legend.*
  St. Louis: Baltimore: Baltimore Sun Co., 2001

WEBSITES

The Baltimore Sun—Cal Ripken Jr.

http://www.baltimoresun.com/sports/baseball/ripken

The Baltimore Sun*'s page on Cal Ripken includes photographs, year-by-year highlights, and updates of what Cal is doing in his retirement.*

Baseball Hall of Fame—Cal Ripken

http://www.baseballhalloffame.org/hofers/detail.jsp?playerId=121222

You can visit the Baseball Hall of Fame's Cal Ripken Jr. page to see Cal's career stats, a brief biography, and a photo of his Hall of Fame plaque.

Major League Baseball

http://mlb.com

The home page of Major League Baseball includes scores, statistics, standings, a history section, and player profiles from past and present.

Ripken Baseball

http://www.ripkenbaseball.com

The home page of Ripken Baseball, founded by Cal and Billy, includes information on baseball camps and academies, news updates, and links to Cal's minor-league teams.

INDEX